MEWL HOUSE

M SARKI

MEWL HOUSE
© 2005 M SARKI

PUBLISHED BY
THE ROGUE LITERARY SOCIETY
LOUISVILLE, KY
mewlhouse@gmail.com

PRINTED IN THE USA
ALL RIGHTS RESERVED
BOOK DESIGN © 2014 ROGUE LITERARY SOCIETY

ISBN-13: 978-0692290637 (Rogue Literary Society)
ISBN-10: 069229063X

This paperback trade edition of **MEWL HOUSE** *was originally published in 2005 by The Rogue Literary Society as a hand-made, limited-edition collection of poems. There were a total of fifty-four copies produced. The book was manufactured using Asian techniques in the shaping of a hand-sewn artifact. The cover was rendered of artisan Canal Paper. The text was laser-printed on twenty-four-pound linen paper constituted of twenty-five percent cotton. Each copy was signed by the author and was numbered in the order in which the volume was produced.*

FOR BEVERLY

Previous books by M SARKI include:

ZIMBLE ZAMBLE ZUMBLE
elimae books 2000
Dallas, Texas
(Handmade limited edition of 75.)

ZIMBLE ZAMBLE ZUMBLE
Author's Choice Press 2002
Lincoln, NE
(Paperback trade edition.)

LITTLE WAR MACHINE
Ravenna Press 2004
Edmonds, WA
(Paperback trade edition.)

TABLE OF CONTENTS

WORD AT THE FIRST

—GORDON LISH

T H E   P O E M S:

Word at the First

Didn't I do this once already? I'm pretty positive I did this once already. I mean: produce a bit for Sarki for it to go up in front of what is thereafter to be found in a book by Sarki.

Fine.

Swell.

I am doing it again. Not because it frightens me to say no to Sarki but because it frightens me for me to fail—asked or not asked—to speak. So to speak for Sarki comes to speaking for speaking's sake.

Which is for being's sake.

It's a test.

It's proof.

All being is. Despite irritating injunctions to the contrary.

Sarki lives and is therefore a poet. Perhaps you don't understand this. But when there comes to you a time of understanding this, take out Sarki's verses and look again at their proof of being.

The test he passed?

Speech—in the manner of almost truth, a command Sarki could not, save if a suicide, elude. You will never find more in a man.

But are you looking?

I mean: for more in anybody?

—GORDON LISH

MEWL HOUSE

M SARKI

When You Start to Dig

I ruptured your bean
and made of it my
plaything. But

how can you know
I did? Look here,
between each vine.

See the way the leaf
peels by means of
the wind? Pivoting

all at once? Sensing
its mission for
spotting my chaff

between them?

The Third Kentucky Lunatic Asylum

I would love to have my picture taken
standing beside this honey locust.
There I am, holding a bean pod and
needled legume while my free hand
rests on the head of my mother who
sits quietly on a rosined railroad tie.
There are lavender flowers
everywhere, stretching out of the tall
grass. Their blooms look like busy
caterpillars, their little legs motioning
eagerly for us. Waving. Blowing
kisses. And beneath the feet of my
long-term gurney the ground is hard
and flat and cuts through fields near
our cemetery. Crazy people die here.
O look! Under the granite and moss
lies Bob. Now that is viminal and hell.
Or dale. Or toggery meant to retard
this poet. But the holy bell am I who
whips his steed past noon and gamely
circles these portals with autonomy.

Confessing

I climbed his fence
to ply again her
congee.

Avowed, she let
me fleece it then;
fourchette and

recompense.

3

The Fall

Thought you should know I dropped
from my roof. Nothing broken but my
huaca of adventure. Also clay pots.
Never climb to great heights on
pebbled gravel, friend. Too beady.
Too readily upset and told to turn
and tremble: the kidneys, the groin,
the spleen of middle age. Took me
forty-six years to find a quicker way
down my hip. No safer bailiwick but
the one my toes are aiming for. Got a
knot on my leg the size of my knee.
Ice packs galore. Laughter in every
uncle's household in America. Phones
ceaseless with news of my great spill.
Would I were high up enough for
agony again.

About the Beaten Side

I eat corn flakes
to stomach the
daily news.

Emollients wash
my meat, and
gullet a scarcity

of my reason.
My underwear
reeks with a thud

and the paint of
a life worth living.
Such is another death

overcome.
So little time
to grieve. Worse

now, the cracking
of home.
The egging

of degrees.

Mewl House in September

It was the beauty of
the date, the clearness
of the morning's
possibility that
destroyed our well-
being. Imagine a fiery
bird hanging from a
word. And a
subjugated sun and the
plumes that made
history. The largeness
of dread, of humanity
scrambling, covered
with dust and the
violence of futility.
Those were anxious
moments before the
sledge and blade. The
polemical sense of
innocence and
provocation. And the
cloud of horror in
the order to go about
our day.

The Nuisance of Glue

Great timbers
fell this morning.
An atrocity settling

as a pile of debris.
That breached
the bag of

our lady.
A lesson for
freedom delivered

this day. The
favor of
no tomorrows.

Tweezers and Gauze, Unguents That Percolate

Why not be bisit?
Everything else being
taken away,

and now he gives back to
Irma the picture of
her perfect tits.

And the one of
the space holding
up her feet.

Their bottoms facing
the terrible ceramic tile,
as if his whistling

were enough song.

8

Names for Language

Sky and howl
and spade.
We hazard

these avenues.
A panache of
longitudes.

Gone these
Lancelots,
to clay.

9

Crazy Taste

That begum is so whole-
some, so propitiously
benign I want to

colonize the lot. My
embouchure on her
breach, my glossa

plunging deep within
the bounds of her
perfect vuln. O

Jesus! — just to feel
this complete. And
plump about my room.

Bouncing on the Node

I want nookie. To
knock about the stock-
room with. We two,

osculating, as worrisome
rain seems to. And then
cramming ourselves into

her smelt bucket.

11

Daniella in the Palace

Grapa knew I was gulping
the warp of her back
leeward to the blut

of her trigon.
And still she willed
herself to lie still,

withstand my
hysterical probing.

Aimed for the tambour.

Held it sconced, she did,
refusing all qontri.

Alphonso's Lamprey

His sediment becomes
my fallen kitchen. A
massacre of fruit

instantly uncharitable.
A loud buck of meat
long-seared and the

milk no person's
drinking. This party
will never surrender.

Even when the banging
dies. His head a raucous
globe and foaming

departure.

13

On Turning Fifty

I do not bet on
the dimensional.
Too prolonged an

operation for my
way of thinking.
Give me, rather,

a taste for its pucellage.
Or a sudden jolt
infused in

fastidious halls. As
in her sister's cranny.

14

Gaffe's Inquiry

It is true she
has me go in the
morning just before

light. Beyond the
wooden bridge.   It
is where I aim

my flageolet
into the vagueness
and where she begins

unraveling. Oh, my
misguided chrism
flattens the wild mint!

Listen. I dismiss the
need for further
supervision.

In the Treetops near the Ocean This Day

I have seen
where gash
and bush

collided.
The squeeze
astride the

knob. My
shadow's
farther up

the stairs.
As collapsed as
my regard.

Cattle Dam

Maybe it was
ankle to chin.
The uniform

tidy in spite of
the fecundity.

He, fleshed and
smoldering
near ash.

His tissue revealed
in each parting

flood of her
proglottis.

17

Climbing a Mountain of Failing

I would have
watched her
come hither.

Play down
her body
and spall.

Such fuss
was the carriage
for bringing

her perfume of
decay and dog.

Ausable

In a wooded slip

outside the harbor
she fits inside
his wooden
sleeve

and hums

harder.

Unhooks the bells
from all her things.

19

Emily

This claddish monk
keeps coming
near her hedgerow,

fondling
that sentimental yeast
while the must

she is saving
falls off her haggard vine.

Hungry

Only a casual reading
could have made
us acquaintances.

One must have
mixed her wine
with these words.

O precious time
of having been
in her fine body.

21

Missouri, Das Unheimliche

Exactly how the cow feigns
her breath is enough for his
inveigling, his thirst mostly

laden even at the prow of my boat,
his teeth trembling for the piece
of her aspis I have hidden in

my pocket.

New Days of Digital Photography

Another song came forth,
exhibiting itself as abundant
photos of a particular get-up-
and-go. And no inequity was
spared my subject necessary to
her performance. She was
splendid. And nothing
prepared me for this excellence.
The blessed phenomenon of a

good wife unmade.

Four in the Morning

She is lost in
the apparatus.
But the strange

can get beyond
a performance.
And live

within that
slippery grip.
It is obscene,

this giddiness,
the naked distance
between garments.

24

The Bells and Bottom of Miss Lane

School taught
Me constellations.
Church, to fear

His rules.
But you are
The muffin in

My paradise.
And I, the one
Who knows

Good food.

Umgebung

I make music
from your arms,
and from your

pretty slash
in order that I
might eat you

just as I do
your noodles.

26

My Breath with a Staple Driven Through

Fraught as God
between these
legs, I hear

Mother in the
kitchen. Father
explains his

day. But I
clean the spout.
And douse my

hocks with bag balm.

27

Sault Saint Marie

What brings a man
to labor
in her house?

Tall glasses rattle
on this shelf.

Water so deep
the reach can make
the tongue spurl black.

And so the tables avail us of
this convenience.

There are orange peels
that must be eaten.

Sinner

Tell how the yellow wood
and scented brook

rues through the night.

How you slip into wild
blues of honey.

Happiness Among Cows

You were swollen
and still I made
advances, exacting

and forbidden.
Your vital response
was incredible,

given the fraud
between your legs.
It is no little wonder

I endured in the
congress of my
burrio. Upright.

Intact.

30

Where All the Angels Do Not Sing

In the wounded flat
the sawyer's
tongue pretends.

What mallow in
her madness
draws the tepid

rush again.
And the fluid
from her basket

welds my chin cold.

31

The Darkness in the Lightness of Her Demitasse

He will lick
the brown fistula
she keeps dangling

as her find,
but his love
is for his cyathus

suspended.

Of Daphne Odora

This dotted stare
In the eyes of her needle,
Of her wooden spools

Given her last ardor,
Her thickened scent
Still orbed on the sofa,

All the ways she looked
Before she left.

33

She Goes Forward

The gardenia headed
for her rose.
And then

she stumbled.
Was forced instead
to shimmer

with that thorn
beneath her clothes.
What wonder

is a woman
in her suffering.

Gangrel's Lading

Surely you know.
Her room is bare.
These white walls

deceive you.
But listen.
Do you not hear

the sound of
his scratching?
Her stylish rat

making hay
whilst our sun
shines?

Everything for Moppel

Packed for years in
Her omentum, he felt dolce
And so queeved himself

Doughy. What had been
Previously noted as a
Superb disposition

Soured on him, fat as
He was. But, fortuitously,
His araneous woman

Exercised him until he
Minimized himself into
A mere speck on the

Flank of one of her smallish,
But now entirely
Sufficient, udders.

Such abundance
The god wanted more of.

Beyond the Glass at All

There are moments,
early, that top
my day. The

fortune of a
world disclosing.
Glimpses subjacent

to the light before
shadows. The
conception of

silhouettes as sound.

Landscape of Bridge

This carat is
my woman. Her
rehearsal flashes

in bulbs and
an amateur
recording.

There are sounds
she makes.
Measures succinct

and clean as
the floor her
body modifies.

She is circled
and dreamed.
Her casing shudders.

Her jibs and
shelves bear out
my memory.

Of mangoes
viciously disturbed.

Unabashed

Restless is the poule
that smothers this bloom.
And so she begins.

First her recourse is
the forelegs, the shims
of its back, and then

down the stem.
Quite eager she is for
the always perpetual
forever.

Planting the refusing.
Looking beyond the
afternoon.

39

Dialing for Dharma

We are civil's warts.
And our feet grace the
parting unmentionables.

In the night air, frogs
tune as fellows, tall,
tell cowards how

we manage. Is
this our lady's wealth?
Her forearms astound you.

40

The Hem, or a Leg on Lincoln

Up north a
season dies on
trees. The

branch is made
a switch for
advancing

abnormalities.
Life sentences
harshly unacquainted

with an inaugural
event. And so,
severely, the

burler comes.
And goes, again,
to his hardtail

folly.

Assisting Our New Stenographer

If I were a man,
I would fuck
you. Cram

myself in deep.
But, no, I am a
lady, peculiar.

I have a beard.
Your hair
in my teeth.

42

Gavelkind

In reverse she will fasten her
bra and turn to look at her
face in the mirror. What
follows is sorrow looking
down the frame to the last
button on her blouse. There
she decides to remove them:
the blouse, the bra,
everything else her life is
made of. She steps into the
cast iron and reminds
herself that her mother
knitted, not out of duty, but
to demonstrate that it was
she who was in charge.

43

North Ontario

She asked if I
wanted her to
do it. Many

came to mind.
There were balls
with pins and

dowels. Fancy
chimes. Hungry
children in the

hall complicating
matters. And I,
there, afraid

of my wife.

44

Jefferson Truck

Why do the scabs
on my feet burn
when you are

less clothed and
I have not mattered?
For twenty years

I paid to hold
these breasts.
And not saved

enough for others.

Scared

The dirt gave
way. And I fell.
The children

laughed.
It was this
faltering.

And the
chance that I
might be made

a casualty.
Different from
them.

But first.

Aristotle

If I were reduced
to an adjective,
I would choose

vainglorious.
It feels right
on the nose

on my personal
tongue. The
way it fills my

personal mouth.
Leaves room
for nothing else.

O, to be oneself!
A simple noun,
and happy.

Peter Tell

Their age is heavy,
and my touch a little
woody to this clan

wishing to rag on
about obligations.
Notice the angels,

along with Jesus,
standing at my door.
For a minute

everybody looks
familiar, as if
I, or sense, had

something or other
to do with it.

www.ingramcontent.com/pod-product-compliance
Lightning Source LLC
Chambersburg PA
CBHW070117070426
42448CB00040B/3098